Teaching the Craft of Writing

Voice

by Lola M. Schaefer

New York • Toronto • London • Auckland • Sydney
Mexico City • New Delhi • Hong Kong • Buenos Aires

Teaching *Resources*

Dedication

For young writers everywhere

Acknowledgments

I appreciate these teachers who shared their insights as well as samples of student work:

* ✳ Marolyn Krauss at Horizon Elementary School

* ✳ Michele LaFever and Carolyn Fletcher at South Adams Elementary School

* ✳ Heather Fox and Hilary Hamman at Pierceton Elementary School

* ✳ Jaime Brunson at J. E. Ober Elementary School

* ✳ Darla Kingrey and Ann Hollar at Horace Mann Elementary School

Thank you to my editors, Joanna and Sarah, who both continue to be a source of inspiration and support.

And, I offer my sincere gratitude to student writers, who willingly experiment and tell us what works best for them.

✳ ✳ ✳

Cover Design by Maria Lilja
Cover Illustration by Kristen Balouch
Interior Design by Sarah Morrow

Copyright © 2006 by Lola M. Schaefer
All rights reserved.
Published by Scholastic Inc.
Printed in the U.S.A.
ISBN 0-439-44398-9

2 3 4 5 6 7 8 9 10 40 11 10 09 08 07 06

Table of Contents

Introduction 4

Chapter 1 ✻ What Is Voice?:
Introducing Voice to Students 5

Chapter 2 ✻ Student Writers and Voice:
Helping Students Develop Voice 10

Chapter 3 ✻ Describing Voice:
Enhancing Students' Understanding of Voice 23

Chapter 4 ✻ Read Like a Writer:
Learning About Voice Through Literature 29

Chapter 5 ✻ Voice and Genre:
Hearing Voice in Fiction, Poetry, and
Information Text 38

Bibliography 45

Introduction

For the past eight years, I have been a visiting writing coach in elementary and middle schools. During my residencies, the students and I create our own original pieces of writing from an initial idea through revision. During this three- to five-day writing process, we are constantly working on craft. Craft is the art of using tools and skills to produce meaningful text.

As I work with student writers, I envision that each of them has a writing backpack. Our job as teachers is to provide children with strategies that become life-long tools they can carry with them in these backpacks. How do we do this? We first create a non-threatening writing community where teacher and students experiment with words, side by side. Next, we offer students a rich environment of published literature, modeling, demonstration, practice (lots of practice), and a receptive audience.

What is so encouraging is that I watch student writers embrace these strategies and quickly improve in the craft of writing. Since writing is a form of self-expression, it only makes sense that they would want to know how to do the following:

- use and maintain a writer's notebook
- select and refine an idea
- organize for different purposes and genres
- add interest and information through elaboration
- develop a genuine writer's voice
- write strong leads that lure readers into the text
- create endings that satisfy readers
- revise the piece until it reflects their intent

I believe that students' attention and commitment are strong because they are practicing craft in the context of their own authentic work. Involvement is always more active when writers are able to self-select their topics. They have something to say that is important to them—something they believe and care about. The writing has a purpose and the strategies hold promise to help students realize that purpose.

Teaching craft is more a journey of discovery rather than a precise, step-by-step program. Student writers need to be immersed in a constant study of how other authors craft their work. They need to study published writing such as poetry, story, nonfiction, and memoir. They need well-focused mini-lessons that act as constant reminders of what craft is and what it can do. They need time to reflect, plan, draft, rethink, draft again, revise, and share.

Most important, our student writers need encouragement and support. Celebrate everything they write well. Then, watch your students express themselves in ways you never thought possible.

Chapter 1

What Is Voice?

Introducing Voice to Students

I'd guess that no two writers would define voice exactly the same way. Some might say it's the expressive part of the work, a combination of the author and the narrative coming together. Others might believe voice is a quiet background music coming from the heart of the writer that's always present. Still others might suggest it's the honesty of the writer working through a character. Even though people may define voice differently, readers and writers agree that it is essential to a strong piece of writing. The voice in a piece of writing provides the emotional connection between author and reader. Therefore, learning how to develop voice is important for all writers, young and old.

Our job as teachers is to explain voice, this element of writing craft, to young writers. After just a few preliminary explanations and demonstrations, I find that students become aware of voice in published work and strive to find their own writers' voices.

The first definition I offer elementary schoolchildren is that voice is the personality of the writer coming through the words we read. In our minds, we can hear the author speaking with us. Just as all of us are quite different people with distinct likes and dislikes, talents and flaws, quirks and gifts, all writing voices are different, too. The one thing they do have in common is that they're honest. Each book, each poem, each piece tells us something about the author who wrote it.

Author Studies

A great way for students to discover the differences in writing voices is through author studies. Lead them into a careful examination of voice in published writing. I like to read three or four books by one author. Depending on the grade level and the literary background of your students, you may decide to read a group of picture books or short chapter books. I prefer to read a mix of both so student writers can hear and recognize voice in many lengths and kinds of work.

I tell students in advance that we're going to study a set of books by one author, and I encourage them to listen carefully not only to the storyline but also to the style of writing, the vocabulary, and how the books make them feel.

I begin by reading aloud several books by one author, one right after the other. For instance, when I read these Judy Blume titles with students—*Tales of a Fourth Grade Nothing, Superfudge, Pain and the Great One,* and *Freckle Juice*—students are able to tell me something about Judy Blume's writing and what they think they know about her.

Here's an example of the questions I ask and the responses from students during an author study of Judy Blume.

Mrs. S.: How would you describe her writing?

Michael: Full of fun.

Levi: There is always something happening.

Joanna: She's silly. She makes me laugh.

Mia: It sounds like our house.

Raul: It's one surprise after another.

Emily: I always want to hear more.

Cody: Her writing makes me feel good.

Mrs. S.: What do you think you know about Judy Blume the person?

Joanna: She probably likes to laugh a lot.

Levi: She likes little kids—maybe even naughty little kids.

Bria: Either her house was busy when she was a little girl, or she visited someone with a busy house.

Isaac: She does silly things.

Michael: She might have young children of her own that she watches a lot.

Cody: People in her family love one another.

Tasha: She likes fun words.

In contrast, when I read aloud these books by Marion Dane Bauer—*If You Were Born a Kitten, An Early Winter, Love Song for a Baby,* and *On My Honor*—students describe the author and her writing differently.

Mrs. S.: How would you describe Marion Dane Bauer's writing in these four books?

Mia: Sometimes it's soft and quiet.

Raul: It makes you think.

Emily: It gives you a feeling way down deep inside.

Neil: It makes you care about certain things.

Cody: The writing is about family, but in different ways.

A Teacher's Voice

A first-grade teacher from an area school was a student in one of my graduate education courses on writing in the elementary classroom. One evening, after participating in literature discussions on voice with a guest speaker, she wrote her own description of voice. She says what many of us feel.

Voice is . . .
Voice is writing like you feel.
A piece emerges
from your heart . . .
from treasured memories
intricately stored in the depths of your mind.
It's YOU!
You find yourself
coming alive
through your pen.
Just the right words . . .
just the right flow
of the meaning
of your experiences.

by Deb Schwartz, 2003

Joanna: Sometimes you feel like it's whispering.

Michael: It's about serious stuff.

Tasha: There are lots of good words.

Mrs. S.: What do you think you now know about Marion Dane Bauer?

Bria: She thinks about things.

Levi: She likes family.

Cody: She probably has children of her own.

Isaac: She really likes babies.

Mia: She thinks people should be truthful.

Isaac: She likes to write.

Emily: She has seen baby animals be born.

Levi: Maybe when she was a kid she made a pretty big mistake.

Michael: She thinks family should stick together.

I am always so surprised by students' descriptions of the writing and what they assume to know about the writer. They are quite intuitive during this process. One reason could be that during an author study we are immersed in that author's work. Students begin to mention similarities between books even as we read them. Their engagement level is high and purposeful.

Another reason for students' insightfulness could be that we're talking writer to writer. I explain that since we are all writers, using the same craft tools as published authors, we need to examine carefully how these other writers engage us in text. If voice is the personality of the writer, we should be able to learn something about authors from their work. I expect students to look critically at the writing and find similarities between the books, and so they do. I'm assuming that as writers themselves they understand some of the background needed to shape a piece of writing—and they recognize this in the work that we read and discuss.

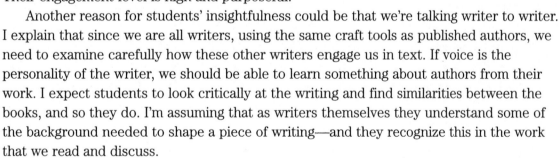

An Honest Writer's Voice

Another way to introduce and explain voice to elementary students is to read them a passage from one book. During this experience, they have an opportunity to listen to an excerpt that displays a specific emotion. They can listen to how an author builds that emotion with an honest voice in one particular scene. Please, select a passage that your students have heard in context before isolating it for this craft study. Of course, it only heightens their engagement if you use an excerpt from a book that you know they enjoy.

> ### Voice Is a Packaging
>
> Ann Turner, author of many children's books, canvassed her friends while thinking of her description of voice. Here's a part of her findings.
>
> *One friend said it is like a color that washes through a piece of writing, or almost like a smell unique to that writing. It is something that marks a poem or novel as yours; no one else could write it in quite the same way. So voice is a packaging, a wrapping up of all the ways in which you use words—your style, how you present dialogue, how you describe far mountains and peoples' faces, and also how you reveal your heart.*
>
> Visit Ann Turner's Web site: www.annturnerbooks.com.

I often use the following section from *Over the River* by Sharelle Byars Moranville, which involves the main character, eleven-year-old Willa Mae:

I slipped out the kitchen door and through the darkness to the truck. Nana and Daddy were coming from the machine shed, each carrying a lantern. I got in the truck and hunkered down on the floor on my side, shutting the door behind me, not worrying that they would hear the noise in the pounding rain.

After reading this paragraph aloud, I ask: *Did those words sound like a computer wrote them, or a person?*

Of course, students generally say that the words sound like a person wrote them. I probe further, asking them to explain their answers: *What makes you say that? Why do the words sound as if a person wrote them? How do the words make you feel?*

Student answers vary; these are some responses I've received from second and third graders:

- They sound sneaky. A machine wouldn't know what sneaky feels like.

- It sounds like this kid's doing something she shouldn't be doing. Only a person understands something like that.

- I feel nervous for her—like she might get caught at something.

- Only people know what it's like to hope you don't get caught. I bet this author has done something like that in her life.

Once everyone has had a chance to respond, I guide students to the main understanding I want them to have of voice. I say: *What you're describing is the voice of the writer coming through her story. Does this writing feel honest and real?*

By this time, all students are in agreement. I extend the point by saying something such as this: *When authors write about something they know, or something that is very important to them, their writing sounds honest, because it is. They are sharing something with the reader that they believe in. Does this writing sound like the author knows what she's writing about—that she believes in what Willa Mae is doing?*

At this point, some students usually begin to express their own personal connections to the writing. After their comments, I remark: *As a reader, if you believe in the writer's words, too—if they seem real and honest—then you and the author meet in the words. You make an emotional connection with him or her in the writing. Do you feel like you've met this author?*

Students have responded with wonderful comments such as these:

- Sort of—I feel like we're both worried that this girl will get in trouble.

- I feel like she knows that sometimes we have to do sneaky things like this, I guess. I feel like I've met her through that.

- The author seems real to me because the girl seems real.

Then, I end by connecting the element of voice to their own writing: *When you're writing a story, whether it's about you or a made-up character, let your writer's voice come through the words. Let your audience hear YOU in your writing. Be honest.*

To recap, voice is the author's personality resonating in his or her writing. It's the emotional connection shared by the author and the reader. It's the honesty of the writing that reflects what the author knows, cares about, or believes. Every bit of voice depends on passion. The author must be passionate about what he or she is writing, or there will be no voice. That's why it's really important for students to self-select their writing topics. To produce strong writing, student writers must invest themselves. To do that, they need the freedom to write what they know or care about. Given the choice of topic and form, their voices will sing through their words.

> *"Voice is like the reader talking through or with the character."*
> — 4th grader

Chapter 1 Review

- Voice is the personality of the author coming through the writing.
- A writer's voice is honest.
- Students can discover voice through author studies.
- The reader and author make an emotional connection through voice.
- A voice is the strongest when an author writes about what he or she knows, cares about, or believes.

Chapter 2

Student Writers and Voice

Helping Students Develop Voice

The voice of a student writer is born with the very first piece he or she writes. However, the child's writing voice has been incubating for a long time. Think about it. Most picture books that he or she has heard have a strong voice. When parents or teachers tell stories, they use engaging voices. As storytellers themselves, children incorporate voice into their own tales. The origin of their storytelling voices is emotion, and they've been developing an understanding of their feelings since birth. Finally, this passion has a place to blossom—in their writing. Young children are definitely passionate about what they know, experience, and believe.

> *"Voice is the feeling or emotion in the story."*
>
> — 2nd grader

As teachers of student writers in grades 2–4, how can we help maintain honest voices in those that have it, or encourage those children who for one reason or another haven't yet developed their own distinctive voices? There are two main ways to accomplish this. First, we need to insure that students can write about ideas that stem from what they know, care about, or believe since we know that's where voice begins. The second way is to model voice in the pieces we write in front of the students.

Writing with Purpose

Student writing must begin with self-selected topics and ideas. We want students to identify what's important to them and to be eager to communicate that with others. The only way that can happen on a day-to-day basis is when students make choices about the subject matter and form of their writing. When students write what they want to say, their writing has purpose.

If we want students to write about what they know and care about, the obvious starting place each year is personal narrative, and that's what I encourage teachers and students to write in the first few weeks of the school year. Sharing the emotional events of our lives with one another helps create a community of writers. I enjoy brainstorming the following topics centered on these emotions with students:

- *Who can think of a time when you were afraid?*
- *When was the last time you were excited?*
- *What's one of the saddest things that's ever happened to you?*
- *Can you think of a time when you were silly with friends?*
- *What frustrates you the most?*
- *What's one of the best things that's ever happened to you?*
- *Do you remember a time when you were embarrassed?*

Students have no difficulty remembering events that are meaningful for them. They become excited about sharing these experiences with an audience. Not only are we learning something about ourselves as writers, but we're also learning who we are as people. We're investing time and energy into each other's personal stories.

Since students are so involved in their topics, the personal narrative is a good starting place to work on craft. And, because their writing is based in knowledge and passion, personal narrative is an excellent time to work on voice.

If students are writing about something that happened to them, then they will know exactly how they felt during that event. They can write with honesty and commitment. I always suggest to students that they hear their next few lines in their heads before they write: *Hear the words, hear the emotion. Is this how you would be explaining it to your best friend on the porch swing? Tell your story with your voice.*

Purpose Makes It Important

Many teachers tell me that they have a difficult time motivating some of their students to write. After asking a few questions, I usually learn that in many cases the students are being asked to write to teacher-selected topics or prompts developed by district writing coaches. As I've mentioned, to generate a desire to communicate for a purpose, we need to allow students to write about their own lives—about what's important to them. Once children learn that what they have to say is important to an audience, they become hooked. From there, we can invite them to explore other forms of writing.

The piece on the next page was one of the first completed by Jon, a third-grade boy, after many starts and stops on other teacher-selected topics. He planned this narrative with enthusiasm because he chose to write about his dog—one of the most important things in his life. Jon worked for three days finding just the right words to describe his pet and the things she does. Afterward, he was anxious to read his piece to an audience. Jon wanted to know what his peers would say in response to his writing. He wasn't disappointed. They listened attentively and provided specific celebrations on what he had written. This audience appreciation was the best reinforcement for Jon. He immediately began brainstorming other topics from his personal life that he could share with an audience.

Jon's passion for his dog clearly shines through in this piece.

My Pug, Vicky by Jon, third grade

When I got my pug dog, Vicky, she was four years old.
Her nose looks like it is pushed in. She is light brown with a black nose.
She looks sad.
Vicky likes to play with her little stuffed horse. When her eyes are drifting
shut, she sucks on the horse's ears.
Her tricks are funny. She rolls and hits a lot of things. She also can spin.
She likes baths in the big bathtub. When she is finished, she runs and
hits things like the phone rack, microwave stand, and the chairs.
Vicky and the family like to ride in Dad's truck and Mom's little red car.
What she likes the best is when we go outside, take off her leash, and let her
run around. We have fun all the time when we are together.

After students have explored the writing process with personal narrative, we can invite them to use other forms to write about their interests. They may choose to write poetry, information pieces, songs, original cartoon strips, science fiction stories, alphabet books, stories about pets, biographies, mysteries, fantasy, or raps. Students need to write using many different forms in order to learn which genres help them express their ideas best. As they practice, they will develop their writers' voices with purpose and intent.

Prompts Rob Purpose and Voice

I'm surprised by how many classrooms are devoting more time to writing from prompts. I know the reason, but it saddens me. Because state and national standardized tests use writing prompts to initiate the performance-based writing sample, many local schools feel pressure to have their students practice with prompts to guarantee success on test day. I certainly understand that teachers want to prepare their students for the testing format—that teachers want students to be familiar with what they will be asked to do. This can be accomplished by taking one day away from the regular writing process each month, or every other month, to plan and write from a prompt.

Easy for me to say, you're probably thinking. I know that there is an extraordinary amount of pressure on classroom teachers to have their students score well on the tests, and that, quite often, funding and educational status in the community revolve around test scores. But we must never lose the focus of our job. We are supporting students as they become life-long, independent thinkers and writers. Our job is to model and instruct them on the writing process and give them ample time to practice, reflect, practice some more, and learn what works for them.

The best preparation for a performance-based test is to give hundreds of authentic writing opportunities in which students self-select their topics. We know that when students write about their own interests, their writing is much more likely to be focused, organized, detailed, and written with a strong voice. They are committed and involved in the writing from the initial idea. That's because they have something to say and want to share that meaning with the tools they know. They have a genuine purpose for writing.

However, if the only classroom writing experiences are centered around teacher-selected topics and prompts, the engagement is limited throughout the practice. The purpose for writing has been sabotaged. Instead of writing to communicate something meaningful, students are expected to write for a score.

When students learn the writing process in an environment of purpose for self-expression, they become astute practitioners of craft. They are quite particular with intent and what is understood by their audiences. Then, when given a prompt, the tools of craft are employed. Students can organize and communicate their thoughts in an engaging manner. In other words, the best practice for performance-based tests is letting students write what they know with passion.

Write Quickly with Passion

One way to help students in grades 2–4 find their true writing voices is by offering them three to five minutes to write like the wind. I've heard this exercise called "Quick Writes" and "Free Writes." Both names aptly apply. We want this writing to be free of worry about form, punctuation, spelling, and evaluation. We also want it to be quick, with no time to fret or reconsider. We want students to tap into the deepest part of their subconscious and let the words come from a true and honest place.

This is how I introduce this exercise:

Today, I want us to take a break and clear our minds of everything. We're going to do something called a "Quick Write." You will need your writing notebooks and pencils. Please clear your work area of everything except these tools. As you can see, I have mine before me. In a moment, I'm going to say two words—just two—and I want you to write those words and then continue writing as fast as you can for three minutes.

There's only one rule—your pencil cannot stop moving. Don't worry about spelling, periods at the end of sentences, or whether what you're writing even makes sense. Just write, write, write. I'll be doing the same thing. And, the great thing is . . . none of us will be writing about the same thing. Please, open your notebooks to the next empty page. Pick up your pencil and wait.

The words we're going to write today are I remember. *When I say go, write those two words and continue writing, non-stop, for three minutes. I'll announce when the time's up. Get ready, get set, go!*

As soon as you say go, you need to be writing along with your students. Continue to write for the entire timed session. Whether it's the first time you've done this, or the twentieth, students will be totally on task, and all you'll hear are their pencils scratching across the paper and the turning of pages. When the timer rings, put down your pen or pencil.

Mrs. S.:   Time's up. Pencils down.

At this point, I often hear groans and some hands will continue moving, trying to complete one last sentence.

Mrs. S.:   Don't worry if you're right in the middle of a sentence. Just put your pencils down. I'd like all of you to go back and read what you've written.

I allow about one or two minutes for students to read. Quite often, they insert words that were omitted in haste.

Mrs. S.:   Now, I'd like you to get in small groups of three or four and read your pieces to one another. If you don't want to share, you don't have to.

I have never had a student refuse to share. I think it's because they've written about something they care about and the pieces are so short. I usually provide five or six minutes for sharing. Watch your groups and gauge the time according to need. The next time, you can have them return to the same groups or find their own partners close to their seats. I always sit in with a group, too, and share what I've written.

Mrs. S.:   This is what I wrote during the Quick Write:

I remember summers at my grandmother's house. I'd wake up in the morning and look out my window to see the Berkshires' blue peaks off in the distance. I'd dress quickly and hurry out the back door, kissing Grandma on the cheek as I raced by. I'd push my way between the hedge and the garage to TaTa's house to see who was up and what was cooking. The smells of fresh oregano and thyme always tickled my nose as soon as I entered her kitchen. If Uncle Norman was awake, TaTa would nod her head and I'd fly upstairs to challenge him to a game of croquet before breakfast. The only reason we played was to see whose ball would get "sent" down the hill and into the creek. (And it was usually me who had to fish her ball out of the icy . . .

After the groups have shared their writing, I gather the class together again.

Mrs. S.:   Now that we've had time to share, let's come back together. Did anyone hear a piece in your group that you think we all need to hear?

Usually someone will volunteer another student with a comment like this, "Go ahead, Drake, read yours. We liked how dangerous you made it sound." I ask two or three groups to offer one piece to the whole class, knowing that the next time I can ask for pieces from the other groups.

Mrs. S.:   We heard some really strong writing today. What do all of you think of Quick Writes?

The answers vary, but these are some of the typical responses I hear:

- I think it's fun.

- We don't have time to really think about it—words just come.

- I didn't think I'd be able to keep my hand going for three minutes, but then I didn't want to stop.

- It was easy to write like this. Are we going to do it again?

- I knew what to write without really even thinking about it.

- I want to add more to this piece. Can I do that later?

What I always notice is that students who might struggle with writing, really get into a Quick Write. It's interesting to see that even students who have difficulty making their letters, write non-stop, undaunted. I know that one day I'll meet a child who won't want to participate, but so far that hasn't been the case.

Another benefit of the Quick Writes is that all students get an opportunity to share with an audience. This encourages interest and positive comments. In fact, many students have decided to expand a Quick Write during writer's workshop because of audience reaction. When peers celebrate a strong lead, specific vocabulary, or recognizable voice, the student writer feels an urgency to elaborate on that topic and write a more developed piece.

The important part of a Quick Write is to offer students two or three word invitations that are personal and to which everyone can relate. I suggest openings like these:

I remember . . .	*I want to . . .*
I know . . .	*I'm afraid . . .*
I believe . . .	*I've never . . .*
If I could . .	*I heard . . .*
I can . . .	*I haven't . . .*
At my house . . .	

One Step More

After your students are into the routine of Quick Writes, you might consider taking it one step further. After they've written for three to five minutes, suggest this:

Mrs. S.: Just for fun, I'd like you to describe the emotion or feeling you get from your writing. For instance, some of you might read your writing today and get a feeling of excitement, worry, joy, sadness, anger, or disappointment. Go ahead and write the feeling that your writing gives you.

Provide two or three minutes for the students to reread and describe the feeling.

Mrs. S.: Now, go ahead and share your writing with your group today. Afterward, ask your friends what emotion or feeling your writing gives them. Let's see if the emotions or feelings are the same or something similar.

Students enjoy doing this extension activity. It will be amazing for you and your students to hear how often their friends describe the voice they hear in the piece in the same way as the writer did. I wouldn't recommend doing this exercise with each Quick Write. Doing it once every six weeks or so will remind students how recognizable voice can be.

You can see the kind of open invitation these words provide. We don't want lead-ins that are too specific because then we would be putting qualifiers on the writing that would inhibit its flow. Don't worry about repeating some of the same invitations; the students don't mind. In fact they often ask, "Can we do the *I remember* writing again?"

Besides encouraging students to write freely with their own voice, some of the other positive effects of the Quick Write exercise, include the following:

- It builds an "I Can" writing confidence in all students.

- Students can use Quick Writes as a source of future writing ideas.

- It reminds students that writing can be exhilarating and fun.

- Students positively reinforce each other's writing efforts.

- Students have an immediate sense of accomplishment.

I usually offer Quick Writes two times a week. Students always ask to do it more frequently, which is good. Keep them wanting more—it helps keep their interest and pleasure high. As time passes, I do increase the amount of time we spend on the writing. Within a few weeks, I increase the Quick Write to five minutes. For second graders, I wouldn't ever make it longer than that. In grades 3 and 4, I usually work up to six or seven minutes in the second half of the year. Again, we want to keep the experience as positive as possible. So, watch your students and don't ever increase the amount of time so much that they would consider a Quick Write a chore instead of a treat.

Also, it's not necessary for students to share their pieces with a group each time. Read your students' needs on that one. Some classes want that feedback. I find that as the year advances, the writers usually don't need the group reinforcement as often.

"Voice is writing for an audience." — 2nd grader

Something interesting to note is that at first most students write about themselves and concrete experiences. Within a month, I notice that more students are writing fictional pieces—even fantasy. When one or two students share their fictional work, it seems to give permission to the others to think out of the box, too. Watch out then! Once they realize the freedom Quick Writes offer, student pieces go in all directions, from talking animals, to short fables, to mini-plays, to poetry. Most important, as you'll see, the writing has distinctive voice. As students experience more freedom and relaxation with Quick Writes, you'll notice stronger voices in their daily writing as well.

Modeling with Passion

The second way we can foster voice in student writing is by modeling it ourselves. Teacher modeling is a powerful tool. Students always continue to do as we do, and sometimes as we say. The support you afford your class by entering the process with them is invaluable. They hear you think, plan, write, read, rewrite, and grow as a writer.

A few years ago, I was contracted to work with several teachers in a school district. One of the fourth-grade teachers was excited about my demonstration lessons but hesitant when she learned that she would be expected to model the process in front of her students. "I'm not a good writer," she told me in private. Yet, this teacher cared enough about her students' growth to take the risk. She began to plan and to write on the overhead projector in class. With little daily practice as a writer, she began the year writing the only way she knew—with a formal, textbook approach.

However, in the next few months, this teacher wrote daily and tried different forms and topics. Before my third visit to her classroom, she met me in the hall. Grabbing me by the shoulders, she shared, "Guess what, Lola? My students said that my writing has a lot more voice now than it did at the beginning of the year!" She was clearly delighted. She was learning and growing with her students. They were a community of writers who felt comfortable celebrating each other's successes—even the teacher's.

It's difficult for writers, even teacher writers, to get excited about a topic that is handed to us. That's why it's important for students to see you, the teacher, self-select topics and refine ideas from your own writer's notebook. Those will be the topics that allow you to use your honest writer's voice. In your demonstrations, let students hear why you select the topics you do.

I like to model this by taking one or two minutes to review some of the entries in my writer's notebook:

> *I could write about how my playful kittens make me laugh, or the time I was stranded out in the ocean in an inflatable raft, or how spring always announces itself in my yard with different shades of purple in the first flowers, or how Aunt Freeda taught me how to pick gooseberries and make a pie when I was nine years old, or my first airplane ride, or the tricks that our dog Thor use to do in the snowdrifts, or the best costume that I ever wore to a party, or the memories I have of bowling with my father on Sunday mornings.*
>
> *I'm in a remembering mood today, so I want to write about Aunt Freeda. I don't think I'll write about the gooseberries. Instead, I want to write about the day that she let me make my first cake. When I pulled the electric beaters out of the bowl, I covered her newly wallpapered kitchen walls with batter.*

Moments from the Past

When entering ideas into your writer's notebook, consider events from your own childhood that hold strong emotional memories. It's surprising how much we can recall about specific circumstances that happened more than twenty or thirty years ago. Sometimes, we have vivid memories about a special birthday or vacation, a certain illness or recuperation, bringing home a new pet or losing one, recitals, reunions, or losing a tooth.

I've noticed that when I write about something from my childhood, students are particularly attentive. I believe it also provides them with additional ideas to add to their notebooks. The added plus is that your students get to know you in another way—they get to meet the child-you.

Let students hear the enthusiasm in your voice as your mind is flooded with memories that you want to capture on paper. Repeating this "thinking-out-loud" procedure helps students know what kinds of entries to add to their own notebooks and how a writer makes decisions on what to select.

Mini-Lesson: Which Piece Has a Stronger Voice?

To extend my demonstration lessons on voice, I like to show students different examples of writing and have them discover which pieces have the strongest voice. I prefer to ask questions and have them make decisions on voice rather than telling them which piece I prefer. In this way, students are engaged and thinking about craft instead of being polite bystanders.

This mini-lesson is particularly helpful when introducing voice, but it also can be used to reinforce voice any time during the year. I begin by writing the same piece in two different ways, however, one piece has a stronger voice than the other. Then, I introduce the pieces to students. Usually, I'll present the stronger piece first as shown below.

Mrs. S.:   Here are two pieces about the same place, but the voice is different in each one.

Share these samples with your class, or feel free to create your own to meet the needs of your grade level.

#1 What Will I See?

One of my favorite places on earth is the creek beside my grandma's house. Why? Because, I never know what I'll see when I get there. Once each summer the town drains the water tower. Thousands of gallons of water gush through the creek, making it look like it's in a race with other creeks to get to the river first. On those days I sit on the neighbor's wooden bridge and dangle my feet. They bounce off the top of the surging water and cool spray tickles my legs. Most of the time, though, the creek is narrow and quiet. Spring water from the mountains trickles over smooth pebbles, sliding down falls that whisper my secrets back to me. But right after a thunderstorm, the creek jumps from rock to rock, playing leapfrog with itself, catching the sun on its back. I'm on my way there now. I wonder what I'll find.

Mrs. S.:   We've been talking quite a bit about writer's voice this year. Plus, you've been doing a great job of pointing out voice in the books that I've read to you. Could someone remind us again what writer's voice is?

Carter: It's the author's personality in the writing.

Lily: Writer's voice is when we hear the author talking to us in the writing.

Imani:	It's the feeling that the reader gets from the words.
Mrs. S.:	How about this piece of writing? Do you hear the author's voice?
Seth:	I do. I hear the writer in the words.
Alisa	The writing has personality.
Morgan:	Yes, it sounds like a kid wrote it.
Carter:	I hear a kid who likes this creek a lot.
Lily:	It sounds like the kinds of things a kid would say about a creek.
Clint:	The beginning sentence makes it sound like a kid wrote it.
Seth:	I think the beginning and ending sound like a person talking to us.
Mrs. S.:	Can you tell me some of the sentences where the voice is strongest?
Alisa:	"One of my favorite places on earth is the creek beside my grandma's house. Why? Because, I never know what I'll see when I get there."
Kristofer:	"making it look like it's in a race with other creeks to get to the river first"
Reese:	"sliding down falls that whisper my secrets back to me"
Imani:	"the creek jumps from rock to rock, playing leapfrog with itself;"
Carter:	"I'm on my way there now. I wonder what I'll find."
Mrs. S.:	Tell me something that you now know about the author from this piece.
Morgan:	She likes this creek.
Kristofer:	She goes to this creek a lot.
Morgan:	The author is telling us how different this creek can look.
Kristofer:	She goes to the creek at different times of the year.
Lily:	The author knows some good words like *gush* and *trickles*.
Alisa:	The author knows how to describe things.
Mrs. S.:	How would you describe the feeling that this piece of writing gives you?
Carter:	It's fun.
Imani:	It makes me want to go to this creek and see it for myself.
Morgan:	I feel like the creek is a nice place.
Seth:	It makes me feel happy.
Carter:	It makes me want to know what the creek looks like today.
Imani:	It makes me feel excited about this creek, too.
Mrs. S.:	Now, I'm going to put the same piece, written a little differently, on the overhead projector.

> "Voice is how the characters speak or feel."
>
> — 3rd grader

#2 My Favorite Place

I like the creek beside my grandma's house. Sometimes it is big and fast. I don't go in it when it's like that. I sit on a bridge and put my feet on top of the water. Spray comes up on my legs. It feels good. Most of the time the creek is narrow and runs slower. Water from the mountains goes over the small stones. Once in a while it drops over a waterfall. I like that. When we have a thunderstorm, the creek goes fast again and jumps from rock to rock. I like to see the sun shine on the water. I'm going to the creek now.

Mrs. S.: How about this piece? Do you hear the author's voice?

Lily: A little.

Morgan: Some of the sentences have a little voice.

Kristofer: It seems like the author's voice is on, then off.

Carter: Yeah, but some of the sentences don't have any. Some are really boring.

Mrs. S.: Read some sentences that you think have voice, please.

Alisa: "I like the creek beside my grandma's house."

Seth: "Once in a while it drops over a waterfall. I like that."

Lily: "I don't go in it when it's like that."

Mrs. S.: Can you please read some of the sentences that you think lack voice?

Morgan: "Sometimes it is big and fast."

Clint: "I sit on a bridge and put my feet on top of the water."

Alisa: "Most of the time the creek is narrow and runs slower."

Morgan: "Water from the mountains goes over the small stones."

Mrs. S.: Why don't you think these sentences have much voice?

Seth: They're blah. They sound like a machine wrote them.

Carter: There's no personality in them.

Morgan: It just sounds like blah, blah, blah—like the author isn't even really saying anything, just writing words.

Imani: I don't hear a person in these words.

Mrs. S.: Tell me what you now know about the author from the second piece of writing.

Seth: Not that much.

Kristofer: He tells us that he likes to go to the creek.

Clint: We also know that he's going there now.

Seth: We know that he's seen the creek look different.

Lily: But we really don't hear that the creek makes him feel excited or happy.

Mrs. S.: Are you telling me that there isn't much emotion or feeling in piece #2?

Hear the Voice!

Bad Day by Tyler Krepp, second grader

One day it was raining cats and dogs. Alex and Tyler got lost in the sewer for two hours. Alex noticed a giant rat on Tyler and ordered him to get it off.

"But, holey moley," said Alex. "There's a rat on your head."

So Alex hit it off and ran after it so he could step on its tail. Good thing they don't give speeding tickets. The rat bit Alex's finger off! Finally, Alex saw a fleck of light. Tyler went with Alex. They got out of the sewer. They asked a man at the end of the tunnel if he had a cell phone. "Yes," he said.

Alex got the phone and called 911.

"Shoot! They put me on hold. Oh, whatever. Keep your phone. Do you know where the closest hospital is?"

"Go straight," said the man, "turn the corner and it should be on your right."

So, Alex and Tyler went as fast as two magnets repelling. But they got there as soon as it opened. They went straight to the counter and asked if there was an available doctor.

"Yes," said the nurse.

"What floor?" asked Alex.

"The 10th floor."

Alex and Tyler ran to the 10th floor. "Hey, Doctor, can you do anything because my friend got his finger bit off by a rat," said Tyler.

Fifteen minutes later.

"Scalpel, please." After thinking, the doctor said, "Can't fix it."

"Rats!" said Alex.

Tornado Damage by Cody Gilbert, second grader

On Sunday, November 10, I was at my cousin's. I was just watching TV. Then the tornado siren came on, then went off. My mom came out of her car. She yelled, "Come on!"

I hollered, "Where to?"

"The fire station!" said Mom.

I watched out for funnels. There were no funnels, but a tornado was about one mile away. I shouted, "Go faster!" We were almost there! We got to the fire station safely.

I flew to the basement and I stayed there. My mom stayed upstairs and I wasn't even thinking about the tornado. After awhile, the tornado was gone.

We went to look at the tornado damage. There were trees down, rooftops off, and windows shattered. So, we went back home and that's when I realized that we didn't have cable anymore.

Conference
by Siairra Sterling, second grader

I need a
conference
right now
or I will
scream!
or yell
or
stomp
or pull my hair.
So, if you dare
yell at me
I will tell you
to
STOP!
and you will freeze!

Kristofer: That's right. It doesn't make you really care about the creek or the writer.

Morgan: It's like you just have to sit there and read it, but you don't want to go to the creek.

Mrs. S.: So, which piece of writing do you feel has the stronger voice?

Lily: The first one.

Imani: Almost all of its words sound like they came from a kid's mouth.

Alisa: It has a personality. Piece #2 doesn't really have that.

Mrs. S.: How do you want to write in the future, like the writer in #1 or in #2?

Students (*all together*): Like #1.

Mrs. S.: So, if I understand what you've told me today, you think writer's voice is when you can hear a real person behind the printed words. You also said that a writer's voice gives you a feeling when you read the words. And, it sounds like you think you learn more about an author who writes with voice.

So you see, the only way that students will be able to recognize, appreciate, and develop writer's voice is if we teach this craft element. Through weekly Quick Writes, students can write unencumbered and "hear" themselves in their writing. If we allow students to self-select topics and ideas during their daily writing time, there is a greater chance that their pieces will have distinctive voices. Our own writing demonstrations and mini-lessons need to focus on voice and the bridge it builds between author and reader. If we maintain these kinds of engagements throughout the year, we will read more and more writing like the examples on page 21.

Chapter 2 Review

- Student writers need to self-select writing topics and ideas.
- Quick Writes encourage honest writing with a strong voice.
- Teacher modeling shows students how to strengthen their voices.
- Mini-lessons that compare pieces of writing help students recognize and appreciate voice and also help their voices become more distinctive.

Chapter 3

Describing Voice
Enhancing Students' Understanding of Voice

Once students can define voice, the next step is to help them describe what they hear. It's difficult to isolate one part of the writing and say that it creates the voice because voice is a collective result of the work. Voice develops with each description, action, bit of dialogue, and individual word choice. Voice is dependent on cadence and style. It's like a mosaic assembled with each decision of the writer. But, when a reader can recognize voice, he or she can then describe it.

As readers progress through a piece of good writing, they become more immersed in the tone of the writer's voice. They hear the tone throughout the piece, like quiet background music, because it is an integral part of the work. This voice comes from both a subconscious and conscious source. Much of who a writer is comes out in voice whether or not he or she is aware of it. But thoughtful authors also make sure that their voices remain consistent, and they establish the tone they want their writing to have. The tone of a voice can be described in a variety of ways such as lively, formal, mysterious, reflective or pensive, playful, compassionate, sober, reminiscent, insightful, relaxing, enthusiastic, regretful, cautionary, persuasive, or zany. We can help students describe voice by teaching them to listen carefully to a piece and to define the mood or emotion that the writing gives them.

> ### Holding It All Together
>
> Ann Turner, novelist, poet, and picture book writer, offers this description of voice:
>
> *If we use weaving as a metaphor, voice is like the strings on the loom on which we weave all the rest of the story. Sometimes it isn't even seen, but it is there, providing structure and unity to the story.*

Listening with a Careful Ear

Students love a good read-aloud, and so do I. A read-aloud is the best place to start helping them to listen with a careful ear. Please, select picture books or passages from chapter books that your students have already heard at least once, if not more. When students have familiarity with the text, they will be able to concentrate on the purpose you provide for listening. Listening with a careful ear simply means that a reader attends to a specific purpose as the piece is read to him or her. The student is hearing the writing through the framework that the teacher provides.

Mini-Lesson: *Waiting for Wings*

Here's a sample mini-lesson on listening that can be adapted to many picture books.

Mrs. S.:   Today, I'm going to read Lois Ehlert's book, *Waiting for Wings*, again. I know it's one of your favorites. Besides enjoying the story again, I'd like you to be thinking about how you would describe Lois's writing. Think of words that will tell us about how it makes you feel about butterflies and their life cycle.

    I read aloud the story.

Mrs. S.:   Can anyone tell me how this book made you feel?

Liam: Happy.

Julia: It made me think that I could fly.

Megan: It made me want to say WOW!

Andre: It made me feel beautiful just like them.

Dillon: I felt surrounded by butterflies.

Kayla: I felt nice.

Mrs. S.:   Lois's voice in her writing gave you those different feelings. She's a gifted writer. Now, I want us to think about this a little more carefully—think about what kind of voice you hear in her words. For instance, I hear her celebrating the life of butterflies. Are there words that you could use to describe Lois Ehlert's voice? When you can name that feeling you get from her writing, you'll be able to describe her voice. Just think of one word you'd like to use.

Omar: Wow!

Dillon: Important.

Naomi: Learning.

Kayla: Uplifting.

Liam: Colorful.

Mrs. S.:   You describe Lois Ehlert's voice well. Can I add a few words, too?

Students: Yes!

Mrs. S.:   I hear a sense of awe, which means that Lois Ehlert thinks this cycle is amazing, and she thinks that if she explains it to us, we'll think it's amazing, too. I also think her voice is filled with wonder. Again, she can hardly believe how all of this works and she's showing us. It's like she's saying, "Can you believe this?"

Dillon: That's what I meant by important. I could tell that the author thinks this is really important and interesting stuff that we should know.

Naomi: I said learning because I think she wanted us to learn what she had learned.

Omar: I said WOW because she makes us think that all the way through the book by the way she writes.

Mrs. S.: Do you think Lois cares about butterflies?

Students: Yes!

Mrs. S.: Do you think she could have written this book in just this way if she didn't care about butterflies the way she does?

Students: No!

Mrs. S.: Do you think Lois Ehlert's voice reflects how she feels about butterflies and their life cycle?

Ariel: Yes, she couldn't write such a good book if she didn't really think all of these facts were interesting.

Jose: We know how she feels because she couldn't pretend that she thought all of this was wonderful. Well, she could, but then her writing wouldn't be fun to read.

Dillon: You can tell this is important to her.

Mrs. S.: What does this mean for you? For you to write with a strong voice, how must you feel about your topic?

Liam: We need to really believe in what we're writing about.

Omar: We need to care about our topics.

Dillon: Important. We should only write about stuff that's important to us.

Mrs. S.: Sounds like you're ready to write today. I hope you all let your passion for what you want to say come through your words. Write boldly and enjoy!

Each Author Has His or Her Own Voice

Author Ann Turner describes her own writing voice like this:

My particular voice—the way in which you know it is Ann Turner writing—tends to have several distinct parts: it is very poetic, including a fair amount of descriptive words. Look at how often the sense of smell is there, particularly the way in which we are comforted by certain smells. Think of Sarah Nita in "The Girl Who Chased Away Sorrow" and how her mother "smells of sheep and wool and wood smoke." I also use metaphors, as in "Abe Lincoln Remembers" when Abe talks about how he learned to "use words/like a leading rein on a colt/to take people where I wanted."

Mini-Lesson: *Owen* and *Lilly's Purple Plastic Purse*

For another mini-lesson to help students describe voice, use *Owen* and *Lilly's Purple Plastic Purse* by Kevin Henkes. This lesson focuses on two books by the same writer. Remember, for optimal discussion and comprehension about voice or any other element of craft, design mini-lessons around books that you have read at least twice to your students.

You can offer this mini-lesson in one day or divide it between two days. Reread one of the books on the first day and ask questions about it, and then reread the other book on the next day and have that discussion.

Here's how a typical mini-lesson might go.

Mrs. S.: Do you like Owen?

David: Yes, he's funny.

Jamaica: He figures out a way to keep his blanket just the way he likes it.

Molly: Oh, yes, he tricks his parents a couple of times.

Mrs. S.: What kind of story do you think this is?

Molly: A story about growing up.

Ryan: A story about something that lots of kids go through.

Haley: A story about how a family can solve a problem.

Mark: A story about making one thing out of another.

Mrs. S.: How did the story make you feel?

Trey: I wanted Owen to be able to keep his blanket. I was cheering for him.

Ryan: I felt nervous.

David: I was wondering how it would end.

Hannah: It made me laugh a couple of times.

Mark: At the end I felt good.

Mrs. S.: What do you think you now know about Kevin Henkes?

Molly: I bet he has little kids at home, or grandkids.

Jamaica: He knows it's hard to give up something you like.

David: He might have a neighbor that's always offering advice.

Hannah: He comes up with funny names, like Mrs. Tweezers.

Mrs. S.: How would you describe Mr. Henkes' writing voice?

You may want to write responses on an overhead or chart paper for reference in the future.

Mark: Sometimes it's silly.

David: Fun.

Molly: It makes you laugh and feel sorry for Owen.

Trey: Fast and funny.

Haley:	Gentle.
Jamaica:	Happy.
Mrs. S.:	I agree with your choices. I also think that his voice honors and respects children. It's like he's saying, "Hey, isn't this kid neat? He just keeps bouncing back and figuring out new ways to keep Fuzzy."

The mini-lesson continues or is carried over to the next day.

Mrs. S.:	Sometimes, one author has a similar voice in other books that he or she writes. Now, I would like to read another of your favorite picture books—*Lilly's Purple Plastic Purse*. As I read, think about how the story makes you feel.

I read aloud the book.

Mrs. S.:	Do you like Lilly?
David:	Yes, she's funny.
Mark:	I like her.
Haley:	She mostly does good things.
Ryan:	Even though she messed up, she's a good kid.
Mrs. S.:	How does this story make you feel?
Ryan:	It changes. Sometimes I felt like laughing, and other times I was worried.
Trey:	It made me feel good when she apologized.
Molly:	It made me feel like everything would turn out okay.
Haley:	It made me want to pay attention.
Mrs. S.:	Do you feel like you know any new things about Kevin Henkes from this book?
Claire:	He must like mice. Owen and Lilly are mice.
Jamaica:	He really likes or believes in families. Both families help their kids out.
Hannah:	He might like kids to draw and write stories, too, because Lilly does that in the story.
Trey:	He knows how kids feel when they mess up.
Mark:	He might have had a teacher he liked a bunch, or maybe once he wanted to be a teacher.
Ryan:	I bet he messed up once in school and had to apologize.
Claire:	He likes to draw mice.

More Books for Mini-Lessons

Here are other pairs of books for students in grades 2–4 to discuss and describe voice.

Always encourage students to compare and contrast the writer's voice in both books. You'll be surprised how many similarities and differences they will mention.

- *Katie's Trunk* and *Nettie's Trip South* by Ann Turner
- *Click, Clack, Moo: Cows That Type* and *The Diary of a Worm* by Doreen Cronin
- *The Gardener* and *The Library* by Sarah Stewart
- *The Bee Tree* and *Thank You, Mr. Falker* by Patricia Polacco
- *Fly Away Home* and *The Wall* by Eve Bunting

Mrs. S.:	So, how would you describe the writer's voice in this book? Is it the very same kind of voice as in *Owen*? Remember, you said that the voice in *Owen* was silly, fun, fast and funny, gentle, and happy. (*Show students their descriptive words from day before.*)
Trey:	His voice in this book is happy, too.
Mark:	It also seems free.
Trey:	I think his voice is fast and funny again.
Hannah:	It's about the same as the last book but a little more wild.
Haley:	This voice is almost warning us—don't do what Lilly did. See what might happen.
Mrs. S.:	I, too, see similarities in Kevin Henkes' voice in these two books. I also think you're correct when you say the voice in this book steps out of the box just a little bit more than in *Owen*. I'd say this voice is a bit ornery and quite playful.

I end the lesson with this comment:

It will be interesting to watch ourselves as writers this year. We might use the same voice in more than one piece. Of course, that will depend on our topics and our audience.

Describing voice is like recognizing your friends on the telephone even though they don't identify themselves. You listen carefully to what they say, the rhythm of their speech, their vocabulary, and any individual mannerisms of style, and then you place a name with the voice. In reading good literature, our mind recognizes cadences, vocabulary, phrasing, and style, and these elements connect us to emotional responses. We can find words to describe what we feel and hear as we read; we know and recognize these emotions and we can put a name to them.

Chapter 3 Review

- Voice is developed by every choice a writer makes, such as description, word choice, action, style, cadence.
- Read-alouds and discussion help students describe voice.
- Comparing two books by the same author helps students recognize similarities and differences in voice.
- Describing voice is putting a name to the feelings a reader gets throughout a piece of writing.

Chapter 4

Read Like a Writer
Learning About Voice
Through Literature

O nce students are writing on a daily basis and discussing the elements of craft, such as ideas, organization, strong leads, word choice, elaboration, and voice, they become more critical readers. They read and reread published literature with more purpose. Not only are they hoping to be entertained by what they read, but now they also are investigating how other authors paint pictures with words, create suspense, introduce characters, and use dialogue to move the story forward. We call this type of careful examination "Read Like a Writer."

As a classroom teacher, you'll see evidence when this begins to happen. Student writers stop reading to jot notes to themselves about a technique or device they admire. Sometimes, they'll copy a short passage from a book that is an example of figurative language, an emotional scene, or a surprise ending. You will also see students taking books to their friends and discussing how an author created exaggeration by repeating a word over and over again, how a poet wrote a whole poem without using punctuation or capital letters, or how an author created animal sounds by using unusual letter combinations. But the greatest indicator that your students are reading like writers will be your observations of the impact on their writing as they experiment with language and technique.

Students do not learn to read like writers all by themselves. Even though their own writing does raise their awareness and appreciation of how other authors craft their work, we need to guide students to look at literature in a new way. We teachers can do this through our modeling. Students need to see what we take away from a piece of published writing. Depending on our involvement in a particular piece, that can vary from day to day. Sometimes, we will note how an author "found" a title for a story. Other times, we'll notice the simile that painted a perfect picture in the reader's mind. And, of course, we will notice the different writers' voices in the pieces that we read.

Another way that we can lead students into reading like writers is during our conferencing time. It's fun to ignite both an idea for format and for voice by showing students examples of published work that's similar to their own. This can be a time to point out the devices that can lead to a playful voice. Or, you might share a passage from a book that has a quizzical voice. Always make sure the books you use during conferencing are titles that students know. Their familiarity with the published work will facilitate a quick and targeted discussion of your teaching suggestion. Finally, working with them to identify inconsistencies in voice and in revising "blah" voices will make their writing voices stronger.

Modeling: Noticing What Other Authors Do

To encourage this kind of experimentation, we need to model, model, model. For example, one day after rereading poems from *Flicker Flash* by Joan Bransfield Graham, I took out my own writer's notebook and made these entries.

- *Try writing a poem in the shape of the subject, like Joan's poems, "Firefly" and "Lighthouse."*
- *Mix facts and fun together in a poem like Joan's poem, "Sun."*
- *Use zippy language, like* ring-a-ding day.
- *Use phrases or words that make a reader think like,* nestled in the lap of night.
- *Try writing a poem with a new voice—one that's lively and silly.*

As I wrote these notes, I told my students what I was writing in my notebook. Then, I invited them to pick up their own notebooks and write phrases or techniques that they heard in the poems to use as reminders for future writing. If you like, you can use a scrapbook or a large notebook as a place for students to record what they notice. Remember to revisit certain texts again and again so students are working with familiar stories, poems, and information. Never ask them to Read Like a Writer when it is their first engagement with that text. Return often to several of the same books or poems and study these to see how other authors work at their craft.

A Read-Like-a-Writer modeling on voice using *Flicker Flash* by Joan Bransfield Graham might sound like this:

> *I've noticed from reading all of Joan's poems that she selects a voice that will complement her topic. For instance, in the poem "Spotlight," she creates a bold, performance voice with her choice of language and her style of writing. However, in her poem "Candle," her word choice and cadence create a voice that sounds like a flicker of hope and warmth. I want to remember that many qualities like format, word choice, cadence, and even organization can influence voice.*

After you Read Like a Writer, make notes in your writer's notebook about voice. Encourage students to do so as well. Samples of my notes appear below.

- *Consider purpose and topic when establishing voice. For instance, a family story about my grandmother when she was a child might have a remembering or nostalgic voice.*

- *A poem about the first snowfall for first graders will have a playful voice of awe or wonder.*
- *Read the book* Scrambled States of America *by Laurie Keller to see how the author developed such a silly, fun-loving voice.*
- *What was it about the voice of* Baby *by Pat MacLachlan that spoke to me so deeply?*

Modeling: Using the Writer's Notebook to Determine Voice

Once all of us—teacher and students—have made notes on voice in our notebooks, we need to show children how we can access them during the writing process. (Of course, the more notes and examples they've recorded, the greater the resources.) It's essential that during the modeling process, we stop and return to our notes. Take a moment to think out loud:

Today I'm starting a new piece. I'm going to write about my favorite memories of my grandmother. I want my voice to represent the pleasant feelings I have when I remember my summers spent at my grandmother's home. I'm going to reread some of my notes in my writer's notebook on voice. Maybe I will find some helpful hints for my voice in this piece.

At this point, you can make a choice. You can silently read some of your previous entries on voice, select those notes that can provide assistance in what you're going to write, and then share your findings with students. Or you can read a few of your entries aloud and let them hear your decision-making process. The example below shows the former choice.

Last week, I wrote a note to myself about how Cynthia Rylant described her grandparents with specific examples in her book, When I Was Young in the Mountains. *Her voice was reminiscent with a bit of nostalgia. That might be helpful since I sometimes yearn for those days when I was a young girl spending two weeks at my grandmother's home. I have another note from last month when I read* Miss Tizzy *by Libba Moore Gray. She described in great detail what Miss Tizzy did with the children in her neighborhood. I heard a loving and playful voice in her work. I could use that kind of voice if I decided to describe some of the things Grandma and I used to do together. Then, when we read* Love Letters *by Arnold Adoff, I made a note that it would be fun to write a love letter poem to someone who is dear to me. I could write a love letter poem to Grandma in my nine-year-old voice, telling her all of the things she does with me that I enjoy. I want my audience to hear a caring and appreciative voice.*

Whenever you're starting a new piece, take about fives minutes to review some of your notes on voice and format in your writer's notebooks. See if a piece of published literature can help you make choices for the kind of voice you want to use in your piece.

Showing Voice During One-on-One Conferences

Another opportunity to use literature to *show* the elements of craft is during teacher-student writing conferences. For instance, if a student is writing an information piece on reptiles and is struggling with finding an honest voice, I might use a copy of *Who Came Down That Road?* by George Ella Lyon and *Trout, Trout, Trout! (A Fish Chant)* by April Pulley Sayre. Both of these picture books provide a narrative treatment of a nonfiction topic. They can be useful to student writers while they make choices about voice and format. And even though students don't usually copy the exact format, style, and voice of a book shown to them during a conference, it helps them think out of the box and develop their own distinctive voice.

> *"Voice is when you hear the author's personality in the writing."*
>
> — 4th grader

Mrs. S.:   What is going well with your writing?

Isidro: I know a lot about reptiles, and I've got plenty of information. I'm using some good words like *scales, lungs, cold-blooded,* and *skeleton.*

Mrs. S.:   Do you have any questions?

Isidro: I don't know how to write it all down. I don't know if I want it to sound like a library book on reptiles or a fun book.

Mrs. S.:   Who do you think your audience will be?

Isidro: Kids—but mostly kids in first to third grade, I guess.

Mrs. S.:   What kind of book on reptiles do you think they would enjoy reading?

Isidro: A fun book. One that doesn't sound like a schoolbook.

Mrs. S.:   I'd like to show you two different ways that you might consider shaping your book. One way to write a book with information is like this book, *Who Came Down That Road?* by George Ella Lyon. This author uses a question-and-answer format. A child asks questions, and an adult in the story answers him. Let's read a few pages together.

At this time, I would pull up a chair beside the student and read the first three or four spreads of the book so he can hear the repeating refrain that the child in book uses:

> *Who came before that, Mama?*
> *Who came down that road?*

The student sees how the author unfolds centuries of history in a simple format of questions and answers.

Mrs. S.:   I'll leave this book here for you to read. I'm curious, though. How would you describe the voice of this book with its question-and-answer format?

Isidro: It's got a "tell-me" kind of voice. You can hear the child asking the questions. The answers make him want to ask the next question.

Mrs. S.: It sure does. I also hear a respectful voice—both for the land and for the feelings the mother and child have for each other. And, I think it has a cozy voice, as if the mother and child are sharing something important and personal to them. You might want to try this kind of writing and see if it works with your information.

Isidro: I could have a child asking reptiles different questions about themselves and the reptiles answering.

Mrs. S.: Yes, you could. That sounds quite interesting—and fun! Or you may want to try another way to share your information. Here's a book that has an unusual format. It's *Trout, Trout, Trout! (The Fish Chant)* by April Pulley Sayre. In this book, the author informs the reader about the different kinds of freshwater fish found in the streams and lakes of North America. But instead of writing complete sentences, she lists the names of the fish in a rhythm that becomes a chant. Let's read the first few pages of the book.

Again, I would read the first three or four spreads of the books to the student so he or she can hear the rhythm and playfulness of the writing:

> *Paddlefish, Flagfish, they're all real.*
> *Mosquitofish, Sunfish, eel, eel, eel!*

Isidro: It makes me want to clap or say the words.

Mrs. S.: Yes, it does have a catchy beat. You could try that form by listing different reptiles and their features. If you chose that approach, you wouldn't necessarily have to rhyme your lines. That was a choice of this author, but it need not be yours. How would you describe the voice of this book so far?

Isidro: It's fun—happy—kind of a bouncy voice that pulls you along.

Mrs. S.: I agree. I'd say it has a playful or lively voice—somewhat like that of a child who is counting to one hundred. As you can see, sometimes the form we select can help us establish voice. Of course, it's always the writing, the passion and knowledge of the writer—you—that creates the final voice of the piece. Good luck. I'll stop back in a few minutes and see what you've decided.

Books with Distinct Voices

These picture books lend themselves to discussions about voice during student-teacher conferences.

- *Book* by George Ella Lyon
- *The Butterfly* by Patricia Polacco
- *The Class Artist* by G. Brian Karas
- *The Cut-Ups* by James Marshall
- *Dear Mrs. LaRue: Letters from Obedience School* by Mark Teague
- *The Dot* by Peter H. Reynolds
- *Freedom Summer* by Deborah Wiles
- *Joey Pigza Swallowed the Key* by Jack Gantos
- *More Than Anything Else* by Marie Bradby
- *The Old Woman Who Named Things* by Cynthia Rylant

I try to limit my demonstration books to two. But I want those examples to offer two distinct voices. I want to open the child's mind to possibilities. During the conference you can have the student write some of his or her thoughts about the books' voices in the writer's notebook. These notes might prove to be a valuable reference on another day.

More Modeling: Teacher Writing

Another way to encourage voice in student writing is to model it ourselves when we write in front of students on the overhead projector. As I mentioned earlier, I always tell student writers to hear what they want to write in their heads before they write it. Younger children sometimes mouth or speak the words before they write. That's good. It lets their inner ear hear the language, and it also provides the opportunity to let their natural cadence and vocabulary pour out of them.

During our modeling, we can show students how writers reread and listen to make sure their voice sounds authentic. For instance, if I wrote the following on the overhead projector, I would ask students for help in deciding if my voice sounded real and if it was consistent.

Mrs. S.:   Before I go on, I'm going to read this section out loud and see how it sounds. I want to make sure I'm using the same voice throughout this scary scene.

I heard noises behind the door. My body froze. My heartbeat pounded in my ears. And then again, the noises—a scraping, a wheezing, a growl. Slowly, I brought my hand forward. But before my fingers could reach the lock, the doorknob twisted and the door opened. I refuse to be afraid, I thought to myself. I am a strong person and I can face any danger that is thrown my way.

My students' hands shot up right away. They already knew where the voice changed.

Mrs. S.:   Ooooh, I heard a definite change in voice. My original voice sounds natural and fearful, but then it becomes almost theatrical, as if someone is reading stilted lines in a play. Did any of you hear a place where the voice changes?

Nick: Yes. Right after the door squeaked open.

Cecilia: Those words: *I refuse to be afraid.* They sound different and weird.

Nasir: Yeah, and the words *I am a strong person and can face any danger that is thrown my way.* That doesn't sound like the person who's been telling the story so far.

Mrs. S.:   All of you have given me great help. I agree. Those two sentences do not sound natural—not like me at all. Here, I'll revise while all of you set up for writing today. I'll try to find that original voice again.

I remain at the overhead projector, trying out new sentences until I'm pleased. When students are settled, I read my revision.

Mrs. S.: Would you please listen to this revision and see if I now have the same voice for this scene? I reread the piece for them with my new ending:
I heard noises behind the door. My body froze. My heartbeat pounded in my ears. And then again, the noises—a scraping, a wheezing, a growl. Slowly, I brought my hand forward. But before my fingers could reach the lock, the doorknob twisted and the door opened. I took a deep breath, pushed my teeth together and narrowed my eyes. Whatever came through that door was going to face one mean-looking girl. How does that sound now?

Jodie: Better. More like a real person.

Zack: It goes together now.

Provide regular opportunities for your students to identify inconsistencies in voice. Write short passages (four to six sentences long) on the overhead or chart paper. Read them aloud, and ask students to identify phrases or sentences that lose voice or do not follow the voice that has been initiated. This is an important group practice that will enable your student writers to assess their own voices in their individual work.

 # Mini-Lesson: Interactive Lesson on Voice

Students enjoy putting natural, kid-like voices on blah passages with indistinct voices. This practice helps them when they are revising their own pieces independently.

Start with writing a stilted passage on the overhead projector or chalkboard such as the following: *Do not go that quickly. I am uncomfortable.* Since voice is dependent on the writer and the narration, you will need to ask these kinds of questions:

- *Does this sound like someone is speaking?*
- *Does this writing sound natural for a student author?*
- *Would a nine-year-old character speak like this if he or she were frightened?*

Then, you can launch into the lesson like this:

Mrs. S.: Can you give me some other ways of writing the sentences that would sound natural for a young character to say, ways that would reflect that the author was being honest about fear—that maybe the author had experienced this kind of fear?

Brandon: Don't go that fast! You're scaring me!

Jodie: Don't drive that fast! I'm scared!

Nasir: Slow down! I'm frightened!

Pete: Not so fast! I don't like it!

Mrs. S.: Depending on the story and the scene, I think any of these would be an improvement. I like how you used the clipped language that shows irritation and fear. People aren't usually overly polite when they're frightened. They tend to get to the point and say what's on their mind quickly.

During discussions, you can write student suggestions for all to see. Another way to involve students is to write a phrase on the overhead projector or chalkboard and have them work independently at their seats to rewrite that phrase with a more distinct voice. Here's a list of some phrases I've used for practice.

- *It was a dark room, and I couldn't see.*
- *Help me. Help me now. I can't move.*
- *I thought it was fun. I'd like to go back there.*
- *I don't understand what you're saying. Could you repeat that?*
- *Oh, look over there. What do you think that might be?*
- *I'm not sure that you're actually telling me the truth.*
- *I'd prefer not to go in there. It doesn't appear to be safe.*
- *I thought the award was going to be mine. I am quite disappointed.*
- *It has not been a good day. Could I speak with you later?*
- *I would like to tell you about something that I saw today. It was so unusual.*

Then, ask small groups of three to four students to share their revisions with one another. (I usually allow about five minutes for the sharing.)

Sharing Voice with Characters

Ann Turner shares this about voice and characters:

I tend to think that our characters chose us—the writers—and tell us how they want their story to be told. One story may start out with the "I" viewpoint; another may start out naturally with the "He got out of bed, put his feet in a square of sun, and cursed the day." You don't know where this voice is going, you simply have to follow where your character leads you.

"Voice" means being quiet; means listening, truly listening, to the tales our characters have to tell us. It means not interrupting, judging, critiquing, or otherwise interfering with the story and telling it in the truest way possible.

Remember, that the purpose of this kind of exercise is to help students find their voices and let those voices come out through the narrator or the character of the scene. Because of this, not all students will respond in the same way. Each one will put his or her own voice on the situation. Just as all of your students' fingerprints are different, their writing voices will be distinct as well.

Chapter 4 Review

- A student reads like a writer when he or she rereads a familiar story, poem, or book to study how the author crafted a particular part of that work.
- Both teacher and students record notes about craft in writer's notebooks.
- Model for students how to make entries on voice in their writers' notebooks.
- During conferences with students, discuss the voice of a particular piece of writing.
- Model writing with a distinctive voice and checking for consistent voice.
- Students enjoy making "blah" voices more distinct.

Chapter 5

Voice and Genre

Hearing Voice in Fiction, Poetry, and Information Text

As I stated earlier, writing personal narrative is usually the first place students find their voices. Their narratives are about themselves or other people and events in their lives. Students have strong feelings about these pieces and usually infuse the writing with their authentic voices. However, the use of voice is not limited to personal narrative.

Voice in Story

Writing story, whether real or fictional, is the next most common form of writing in which you find a student's true voice. Children have heard story since an early age, if not in literature, then surely in the telling of family stories, some television shows, movies, and cartoons. Story has been a part of their daily lives. They expect voice in story and will typically include it in their own writing unless they've seen textbook expository writing modeled.

In story, it is sometimes difficult to separate the voice of the writer from that of the main character. The reader makes a connection with the protagonist and emotionally follows him or her through the story. In *Freedom Summer* by Deborah Wiles, the reader is immediately lured into the friendship between the young narrator and his buddy John Henry. We are excited with and for them as they do chores and run to Fiddler's Creek for a quick swim. We listen as they describe one another, picturing not only what these boys look like but also feeling their mutual respect.

Later in the story, the reader is just as anxious as the boys are that they will be the first ones at the town pool when it "opens tomorrow to everybody under the sun,

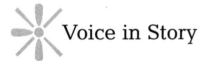

"Voice pulls the story together."

— 4th grader

no matter what color." We ride this wave of anticipation until the next day when they "race each other over the last hill and . . ." The reader stops abruptly, just as the boys do when they see county dump trucks filling the empty pool with steaming asphalt. Disappointment. Anger. Defeat. The reader feels each one of these emotions as the characters reveal their outrage. Finally, the boys share what they want for their future. The reader feels the same conviction and quietly cheers as the boys find the strength to face bigotry head-on on the last page.

Strong and True Voice

Claire Ewart, the author and illustrator of several picture books, including *Fossil, Time Train,* and *The Biggest Horse I Ever Did See*, explains how in *The Giant* her voice and that of her narrator blend to make a story "real."

In much the same way that favorite texts become inseparable from the unique illustrations that give them wings, I believe that a story soars in our minds when its voice is individual and authentic.

In my picture book The Giant *the lyrical, poignant voice of the young girl narrator, thus of the story, contrasts almost immediately with the curt, clipped tone of her Pa, creating tension that carries right through the book's resolution. For me, this particular story of loss and hope set in a rural landscape could not have been told in any other way.*

Young readers are drawn to stories with a strong and true voice, even though they may not know quite why, and even though we might have a difficult time explaining the sometimes nebulous concept of voice.

Better than explaining, we can show them how voice makes a story "real." With a favorite text we may demonstrate how fundamentally changed the text would be using a different voice. When we let young readers hear the difference, they may begin to feel the power of voice, and see it in their minds.

Going one step further, we can encourage young readers and writers to experiment with voice on their own. Then, they will begin to find the unique language that will make their own writing soar!

Visit Ms. Ewart's Web site at www.claireewart.com to learn more about her and the books she writes and illustrates for children.

Throughout this book, we hear Deborah Wiles, but her beliefs are presented to us by her characters. Or are the characters presenting their story through the author? When written well, story is a blend of voices that's too intertwined to separate. Why should we try to separate them? It's a pleasure, both literary and emotional, to be carried through the story by a voice so strong and honest that we never doubt its truth.

In *The Giant* by Claire Ewart, readers are introduced to the young narrator's voice on the first few pages. She misses her mama and remembers her mama's words that giants would look after her.

The reader begins searching for the same giants as the girl—giants, strong and tall. The author/illustrator provides hints of giants, in the sky and clouds, in shadow, and in Pa's manner and work. But just as the narrator wants proof, so does the reader. Again, it is almost impossible to separate the author's voice from that of the protagonist. Whose voice came first?

Finally, as the book nears its end, the narrator's search is complete and so is the reader's. The girl's voice changes from one of wonder and worry to a voice safe and comforted.

> *Now I know*
>
> *what Mama said I'd know.*
>
> *A giant is looking after me.*

Do we hear only the narrator? No, we hear the author allaying her own fears, too, as she thinks of those people who are her giants, who give her peace. Character-driven stories are rich formats for voice. From *Winnie-the-Pooh,* to *Frog and Toad,* to *Wilbur and Charlotte,* students are immersed in the power of an honest voice. We need to continue to share the best literature with our students so they have good models and our permission to write boldly and to find their voices in story.

Voice in Poetry

Poetry does not often have the luxury of character and space, as story does, to develop voice. Yet, the best poetry is brimming with voice. Through repeated readings and mini-lessons, students will hear and begin to imitate what masters have done for centuries. Since most poetry for children uses an economy of words, it provides a short, rich setting in which to study voice.

Poetry That Sings with Voice

Here are a few collections of poems that can lead to healthy discussions about voice.

- *Brown Honey in Broomwheat Tea* by Joyce Carol Thomas

- *The Dream Keeper and Other Poems* by Langston Hughes

- *Hummingbird Nest: A Journal of Poems* by Kristine O'Connell George

- *Joyful Noise: Poems for Two Voices* by Paul Fleischman

- *A Lucky Thing* by Alice Schertle

Place a poem such as "Bumble Bee" by Margaret Wise Brown on the overhead projector or write it out on chart paper for everyone to see and read. In less than fifty words, the poet connects with us emotionally in the bee's world. Students will tell you that they hear a questioning voice, a fun and playful voice. I like to point out that the poet is celebrating the freedom of a bee. I hear almost a wishful voice as she describes what the bee does and where it travels. This voice helps us release our own desires to wander and, sometimes, zoom away, too.

In X. J. Kennedy's poem entitled "Martin Luther King Day" (from *LIVES: Poems About Famous Americans* selected by Lee Bennett Hopkins) it's the cadence, the vocabulary, and what the poem says that blends together to create a voice of honor and remembrance.

In many of Doug Florian's poems, you will find a playful, childlike voice. Here, in his lead poem "Summersaults," from the book of the same name, letters play as much as the imagery.

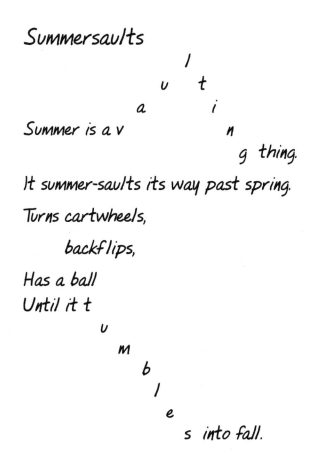

From SUMMERSAULTS by Douglas Florian. Copyright (c) 2002 by Douglas Florian. Used by permission of HarperCollins Publishers.

It only makes sense that poetry would have voice. A poem begins with the unusual. If the poet first marvels at what he or she sees, feels, hears, discovers, or knows, then the poem will carry that emotion to the reader.

Voice in Information Writing

Years ago, it used to be that all information books were rather dry and written in the style of a textbook. Voice was difficult to find in these books. They were straight expository writing without much variation in tone. Today, many of the information books for children are written with a narrative style. These books are jam-packed with voice, and that voice pulls young readers into their pages. Such books can be strong examples of what students can write to share what they know. *So You Want to Be an Inventor?* by Judith St. George offers a lively, "can-you-believe-it?" voice as she shares fact after fact about several groundbreaking inventions and the people who created them. Without giving the reader an entire biographical sketch, St. George sifts out just the strongest nuggets to make the reader say, "WOW, that is unbelievable!"

In *The Flag We Love* by Pam Munoz Ryan, the history, purpose, customs, and celebrations of the flag of the United State of America are presented to the reader. The author's voice is one of reverence and respect. We hear it both in Ryan's verse and in the informational notes placed on each spread.

Kimberly Brubaker Bradley uses a lively, fast-paced voice in her book *POP! A Book About Bubbles.* The author guides the reader effortlessly through information about gas, air, liquids, and soap. Students are intrigued with this celebration of backyard science. The voice disguises the vast amount of factual information being presented, and young readers come back to this book again and again. Student writers can study this book to write with a similar voice about their own scientific interests.

In *One Is a Snail, Ten Is a Crab*, April Pulley Sayre uses an investigative and playful voice to show mathematical groupings using the feet of people and animals. Even though the text is extremely sparse, the reader takes the time to enjoy the unique equations, like "50 is five crabs or ten dogs and a crab." Thanks to the author's voice, the combination of

> *"Authors add their own expression in the writing. That's voice."*
>
> — 4th grader

Voice in Narrative Nonfiction

These information books offer strong, unique voices.

- *Animal Dads* by Sneed B. Collard III
- *The Boy on Fairfield Street: How Ted Geisel Grew Up to Become Dr. Seuss* by Kathleen Krull
- *Sea Clocks* by Louise Borden
- *An Interview with Harry the Tarantula* by Leigh Ann Tyson
- *My Name Is Georgia* by Jeanette Winter
- *Thomas Jefferson: A Picture Book Biography* by James Cross Giblin
- *William Shakespeare & the Globe* by Aliki

math and science (number of feet on snails, insects, crabs, mammals, and spiders) becomes a game that keeps the reader involved in the unraveling puzzle.

No matter what the genre, examples with a strong voice can be found. Students need to see how other authors bring themselves to the page. Through examination and discussion, they will gain confidence to experiment with their own voices in a variety of genres. Let's make sure that can happen by offering them a wide range of excellent reading material.

Chapter 5 Review

- Students can discover and use voice in different genres.
- In story, the author's voice and the character's voice often meld. The voice also connects author and reader with an emotional bond.
- Poems have a variety of voice as well as topics.
- Students can develop their own narrative voices in information writing.

Final Thoughts: The Personal Touch

Every day, teachers around the world are working diligently to inspire and teach students about the writing process. They read professional literature, dialogue with colleagues, and attend conferences, constantly searching for stronger methodology. They want to ignite a passion in student writers that will continue to burn brightly for a lifetime.

To do this, we need to return to the one true purpose of writing—self-expression. Only when we can keep this as our focus are we able to direct students back to themselves, asking them to reach down deep inside and find what's important to them and share that with others. We cannot just tell students this, we must model it. As teachers, we need to write about what's important to us. Then, our practice not only tells the students that we value personal topics and interests, but it also shows them through our own example.

While writing passionately, our own honest writers' voices will emerge. The more the students read this kind of sincere work in our writing and in the published pieces we share, the easier it becomes for them to find their own writers' voices. It is at this point of the process that a community of writers comes together. The words connect us—authors and readers, readers and authors—and our writing grows stronger and more honest.

That's voice. It's the personal touch that we inject into our words. Invite your students to discover their author voices by choosing to write about what's important to them each and every day.

Bibliography

Adoff, Arnold. *Love Letters.* New York: The Blue Sky Press, Scholastic, 1997.

Aliki. *William Shakespeare & the Globe.* New York: HarperCollinsPublishers, 1999.

Bauer, Marion Dane. *An Early Winter.* New York: Clarion Books, 1999.

Bauer, Marion Dane. *If You Were Born a Kitten.* New York: Simon & Schuster Books for Young Readers, 1997.

Bauer, Marion Dane. *Love Song for a Baby.* New York: Simon & Schuster, 2002.

Bauer, Marion Dane. *On My Honor.* New York: Bantam, Doubleday, Dell Books for Young Readers, 1987.

Blume, Judy. *Freckle Juice.* New York: Simon & Schuster, 1984.

Blume, Judy. *Pain and the Great One.* New York: Bantam, Doubleday, Dell Books for Young Readers, 1985.

Blume, Judy. *Superfudge.* New York: Dutton, 2002.

Blume, Judy. *Tales of a Fourth Grade Nothing.* New York: Dutton, 2002.

Borden, Louise. *Sea Clocks.* New York: Margaret K. McElderry Books, 2004.

Bradby, Marie. *More Than Anything Else.* New York: Orchard Books, 1995.

Bradley, Kimberly Brubaker. *POP! A Book About Bubbles.* New York: HarperCollinsPublishers, 2001.

Brown, Margaret Wise. *Bumble Bee.* New York: HarperFestival, 1999.

Bunting, Eve. *Fly Away Home.* New York: Clarion Books, 1991.

Bunting, Eve. *The Wall.* New York: Clarion Books, 1990.

Collard, Sneed B. *Animal Dads*. Boston: Houghton Mifflin Company, 1997.

Cronin, Doreen. *Click, Clack, Moo: Cows That Type*. New York: Simon and Schuster Books for Young Readers, 2000.

Cronin, Doreen. *The Diary of a Worm*. New York: HarperCollins Publishers, 2003.

Ehlert, Lois. *Waiting for Wings*. San Diego: Harcourt, Inc., 2001.

Ewart, Claire. *The Giant*. New York: Walker and Company, 2003.

Fleischman, Paul. *Joyful Noise: Poems for Two Voices*. New York: Harper & Row, Publishers, 1988.

Florian, Doug. *Summersaults*. New York: Greenwillow Books, 2002.

Gantos, Jack. *Joey Pigza Swallowed the Key*. New York: Farrar, Straus & Giroux, 1998.

George, Kristine O'Connell. *Hummingbird Nest*. San Diego: Harcourt, Inc., 2004.

Giblin, James Cross. *Thomas Jefferson: A Picture Book Biography*. New York: Scholastic, Inc., 1994.

Graham, Joan Bransfield. *Flicker Flash*. Boston: Houghton Mifflin Company, 1999.

Gray, Libba Moore. *Miss Tizzy*. New York: Simon & Schuster Books for Young Readers, 1993.

Henkes, Kevin. *Owen*. New York: Greenwillow Books, 1993.

Henkes, Kevin. *Lilly's Purple Plastic Purse*. New York: Greenwillow Books, 1996.

Hopkins, Lee Bennett. *LIVES: Poems About Famous Americans*. New York: HarperCollinsPublishers, 1999.

Hughes, Langston. *The Dream Keeper and Other Poems*. New York: Alfred A. Knopf, 1994.

Karas, G. Brian. *The Class Artist*. New York: Greenwillow Books, 2001.

Keller, Laurie. *The Scrambled States of America*. New York: Henry Holt and Company, 1998.

Krull, Kathleen. *The Boy on Fairfield Street: How Ted Geisel Grew Up to Become Dr. Seuss*. New York: Random House Books for Young Readers, 2004.

Lyon, George Ella. *Book.* New York: DK Publishing, Inc., 1999.

Lyon, George Ella. *Who Came Down That Road?* New York: Orchard Books, 1992.

Marshall, James. *The Cut-Ups.* New York: Viking Penguin, Inc., 1984.

MacLachlan, Pat. *Baby.* New York: Delacorte Press, 1993.

Moranville, Sharelle Byars. *Over the River.* New York: Henry Holt and Company, 2002.

Polacco, Patricia. *The Bee Tree.* New York: Philomel Books, 1993.

Polacco, Patricia. *The Butterfly.* New York: Philomel Books, 2000.

Polacco, Patricia. *Thank You, Mr. Falker.* New York: Philomel Books, 1998.

Reynolds, Peter H. *The Dot.* Cambridge, MA: Candlewick Press, 2003.

Ryan, Pam Munoz. *The Flag We Love.* Watertown, MA: Charlesbridge, 1996.

Rylant, Cynthia. *The Old Woman Who Named Things.* San Diego: Harcourt, Brace & Company, 1996.

Rylant, Cynthia. *When I Was Young in the Mountains.* New York: Dutton, 1982.

St. George, Judith. *So You Want to Be an Inventor?* New York: Philomel, 2002.

Sayre, April Pulley. *One Is a Snail, Ten Is a Crab.* Cambridge, MA: Candlewick Press, 2003.

Sayre, April Pulley. *Trout, Trout, Trout! (A Fish Chant).* Chanhassen, MN: NorthWordPress, 2004.

Schertle, Alice. *A Lucky Thing.* San Diego: Browndeer Press., 1999. 1997.

Stewart, Sarah. *The Gardener.* New York: Farrar, Straus, Giroux, 1997.

Stewart, Sarah. *The Library.* New York: Farrar, Straus, Giroux, 1995.

Teague, Mark. *Dear Mrs. LaRue: Letters from Obedience School.* New York: Scholastic Press, 2002.

Thomas, Joyce Carol. *Brown Honey in Broomwheat Tea.* New York: HarperCollinsPublishers, 1993.

Turner, Ann. *Katie's Trunk.* New York: MacMillan Publishing Company, 1992.

Turner, Ann. *Nettie's Trip South.* New York: MacMillan Publishing Company, 1987.

Tyson, Leigh Ann. *An Interview with Harry the Tarantula.* Washington, D.C.: National Geographic, 2003.

Wiles, Deborah. *Freedom Summer.* New York: Atheneum Books for Young Readers, 2001.

Winter, Jeanette. *My Name Is Georgia.* San Diego: Harcourt Brace & Company, 1998.